Reaching The Hurting

A Biblical Guide For Helping Abuse Victims

Samantha Nelson

Samantha Nelson

Psalm 37

Published by Amazing Facts, Inc.
P. O. Box 1058
Roseville, CA 95678-8058
800-538-7275

Unless otherwise noted, all Scripture references are quoted from the King James Bible.

Cover Design by Steve Nelson
Text Design by Greg Solie – Altamont Graphics

Library of Congress Cataloging-in-Publication Data
Nelson, Samantha.
Reaching the hurting ... : a biblical guide for helping abuse victims / by Samantha Nelson.
p. cm.
ISBN 1-58019-209-2 (alk. paper)
1. Christian women--Religious life. 2. Abused women--Religious life. 3. Victims of crimes--Religious life. 4. Spiritual healing. I. Title.

BV4527.N42 2006
261.8'327--dc22

2006013195

06 07 08 09 10 • 5 4 3 2 1

DEDICATION

This book is dedicated to my Lord and Savior, Jesus Christ. It is my desire that He will use it to reach many hurting hearts and to bring hope, healing, and comfort to those who have been abused in some form.

I thank you, Lord, for all you have done in my life, for the talents you've given me, for the opportunities you've provided me to serve you and others, and for the many ways in which you have drawn me to you with your everlasting love and tender kindness. I thank you for teaching me truth and imparting to me your divine wisdom. I surrender all to you.

To God alone be the glory.

Special Thanks

I thank Steve, my husband, for his never-failing love and support during our darkest hours and our happiest moments.

Steve, you are my greatest blessing, a treasure I will always cherish. Thank you for your steadfastness, your love for God and others, and for sharing your love and life with me. You complete me. I am truly blessed.

Foreword

Understanding that abuse can occur in the lives of both males and females (abuse is not gender-specific), I have chosen to write from a female perspective, using feminine pronouns, as that is easiest for me to do. I believe, however, that the material herein is written in such a way that the male reader will be able to place himself in the scenarios discussed. At times I have used "we" because some principles are applicable to humanity in general, and I have been a victim of abuse as well.

While this book takes a more technical and no-nonsense approach to understanding abuse and helping victims, I don't wish to minimize, in any way, legitimate pain and suffering. A victim of abuse, whether from domestic violence, rape, incest, professional exploitation, pastoral misconduct, or any other source *must* be treated with compassion, love, and understanding. Abuse must not be allowed to continue or to be minimized. We must not tell the victim to just "get over it and move on."

True healing comes from God alone, and it is my prayer that as you read this book, you will begin to understand it is the power of the Word of God that brings comfort, hope, and healing to the victim—not man's theories and labels. Psalm 119:50: "*This is my comfort in my affliction: for thy word hath quickened me.*"

While I have great respect for the genuine science of psychology, I fear too often we have been subjected to (and have unfortunately accepted) unproven, unscientific, and unbiblical theories in place of truth, God's Word, and actual science. I take the counsel and warning in Colossians 2:8 seriously: "*Beware lest any man spoil you through philosophy and vain deceit, after the tradition of men, after the rudiments of the world, and not after Christ.*"

Time and again, I have seen people accept the label that secular, humanistic psychologists have placed on them and, as a result, they attempt to go no higher than the label indicates. They consider themselves doomed to this or that "disease," "addiction," or "syndrome." They are locked into this new line of thinking, regardless of what Scripture states. Frequently, these so-called addictions, syndromes, and diseases are nothing more than a way to sanitize sin. Victims tend to feel they can no longer be responsible or accountable for any of their actions because they have "this or that" problem. Their lives do not improve much, if at all. They continue to suffer and to be in pain. I believe we actually rob people of their dignity when we say they are incapable of making choices—whether good or bad—and are, therefore, not responsible for their own behavior. After all, God bestowed free will upon each of us.

This book was written in part to help counteract some of the problems that can be created in a victim's life when she depends solely on secular psychology instead of a "*thus saith the Lord.*" Thus, this book will be most helpful to those who have faith in Scripture and a desire to have a deeper relationship with the Lord so that they can become whole.

This book is written to assist adults in their process of overcoming pain from their past wounds. The suggestions contained herein are not necessarily applicable, or appropriate, for children or adolescent victims.

I must warn those who may become overzealous or impatient: *This book is not to be used as a weapon against victims and those struggling to do what is right!* We must meet people where they are in their current stage of healing. We must advance only as fast as they can grasp the concepts and incorporate the changes into their lives. We must gently, lovingly, and compassionately teach them and lead them to Jesus—our Great Physician.

I do not recommend randomly quoting Scripture to victims and expecting them to understand and to do what is right. In many instances, such as in a case of childhood incest where the victim, as an adult, is seeking help and answers, the victim has done nothing wrong but has been subjected to violence or abuse due to another's sin. I will cover the responsibility, if there is any, of someone abused as an adult in a later chapter.

For any of us to be of genuine help to someone who has suffered abuse, we must first make sure our own sins are confessed and forgiven, that our relationship with the Lord is right, and that we are able to draw near to those suffering individuals God has placed in our lives with compassion, tact, and tenderness of heart toward them.

Our own motives for desiring to help must be pure. We must not desire to help others as a means of fulfilling our own needs (*e.g.*, to be needed, loved, etc.). We must help others because we love them and have compassion for them. As we gain their trust and prove ourselves their friend by having a genuine interest in their eternal life, then, *and only then*, should we try to help them see what God has to say about sin and suffering, confession and repentance, forgiveness and eternal life, hope, and healing.

It is my prayer that you will use the knowledge you gain here wisely, and that you would softly and tenderly seek to "*bind up the brokenhearted*" (Isaiah 61:1) and restore their faith in their Redeemer.

Table of Contents

Reaching the Hurting— A Biblical Guide for Helping Abuse Victims

Introduction

Reaching the Hurting—A Biblical Guide for Helping Abuse Victims

This book is the result of my personal study (experiential, educational, observational) of abuse and its effects on individuals, and how various treatment methods, thinking processes, and beliefs play a key part in the healing process—or lack of it. Throughout this book I will refer to counselors and counselees. This does not necessarily mean a licensed counselor (psychologist, therapist, psychiatrist, etc.) and someone who is in a contractual counseling relationship with one. The Bible tells us in 2 Timothy 4:2 to "*reprove, rebuke and exhort*," and in Galatians 6:2 to "*Bear ye one another's burdens, and so fulfil the law of Christ.*" This means we are all, licensed or not, counselors to one another.

That being clarified, there is a key point I think is crucial for all counselors and victims to understand—the difference between being victimized without being responsible for anything (as in the case of a child who is molested) and being victimized but understanding and accepting the responsibility we have for our own lives and choices after the fact. This topic is quite "fuzzy" to most victims and, I dare say, to many counselors.

And last, Bible studies have been included at the end of each chapter. These studies are intended for use by actual victims and, in the case of a counselor reading this book for the purpose of helping another, can be shared with those the counselor seeks to help.

Chapter One

What Is a Victim?

As the belt struck the back of her legs again, she sent up a silent prayer, "Oh God, that's the third hit. Why doesn't it stop?" She was accustomed, even at the age of 16, to receiving the usual three lashes of the belt anytime her stepfather was unhappy about something, whether it had anything to do with her or not. This time, however, the lashes didn't stop at three.

No one would deny that being beaten repeatedly with a belt constitutes abuse. That is not normal or proper discipline. The young woman in this narrative is an actual victim of physical abuse. The definition of "victim" can be simply stated as "one who has been harmed by a person, an institution, or by circumstances, to the extent that healthy growth is hindered and maturation is stifled."[1]

According to Dr. Tana Dineen, licensed psychologist, educator, author, member of both the American and Canadian Psychological Associations, and someone who has taken up the task of calling the "psychology industry" to accountability, "'*victim,' once a term reserved for those who suffered from a calamity of nature, of 'Fate,' or of violent crime, now has become psychologized so that it can be applied broadly to anyone and everyone who knowingly, or unknowingly, has been exposed to or experienced stress, distress or trauma. Symptoms such as unhappiness, boredom, anger, sadness, and guilt, can now all be interpreted as signs of prior trauma, creating victims.*"[2] We will discuss this more in a moment.

Unfortunately, in the psychological setting, quite often victims are taught that if they have been abused they are not responsible for their resulting actions, attitudes, or feelings. They are allowed, even encouraged at times, to wallow in self-pity (sadly, some never leave this horrible pit) and keep their attention focused on self rather than on God. What an offense to the true victim and the God-given reasoning powers with which God has endowed every human being! What an affront to the victim who has worked hard to overcome every setback and trauma in life and who has succeeded, by the grace of God, to live a fulfilling life despite less-than-desirable circumstances!

When true victims are shown this kind of disrespect and "fabricated" victims are held to an equal status with those who have suffered terrible trauma, we do a severe injustice to all.

As mentioned, some of the characteristics present in people who are or have been victims of trauma include anger, depression, guilt, anxiety, fear, repeated abuse, abuse of others, physiological problems, identity struggles, eating disorders, promiscuity, inability to enjoy activities, and relationship problems. The list goes on.

Truthfully, though, all these characteristics can be exhibited in otherwise healthy, "normal" but sinful people who have never been abused or traumatized in any capacity. Certain annoying emotions or disturbing feelings are part of everyday life and should not be considered a "sign" or absolute indicator of past abuse or trauma. There is no need for a victim to remain in a state of fear, depression, guilt, or any of the other emotions or behavior patterns mentioned when the Word of God offers abundant life through Christ Jesus. As we continue, you will learn how to apply biblical principles to your life and how to help those who are suffering to apply them to their own lives.

Types of victimization are just about endless, but the ones most often identified include physical, verbal, sexual, emotional, and spiritual abuse. Take, for example, the woman who suffers domestic violence at the hand of her husband but stays in the relationship and home because she has children and is dependent upon her husband's financial support or is too fearful to leave due to his threats. Domestic violence is a crime. She is a victim. But she doesn't have to remain that way. There's the woman who is attacked and raped at knifepoint while getting into her car after work one night. Surely, she is a victim. But there is hope and healing available for her as well. Or take the man who is constantly belittled, hit, and degraded by his wife. He is a victim too. There is hope for him. He can overcome the degradation he has suffered and live a productive life. Then there's the couple who go to church and, after months of grooming, fall prey to a predatory pastor (fortunately this is the rarity, not the norm) who nearly destroys their marriage by seducing and abusing the wife and trying to convince her to leave her husband. They suffered abuse as well—spiritual, emotional, and sexual abuse. In the professional community it is called exploitation. In the faith community it is called misconduct. Is there hope for them to be able to attend church again or to trust in God again? Yes, I believe so. I *know* so.

Now in contrast, let's look at the man who gets fired for poor performance on the job. He claims he is the "victim" of some conspiracy. Is he truly a victim in the genuine meaning of the word? No, I think not. Or what about the couple who are having a heated argument when the husband thoughtlessly says something derogatory, something he would normally never say to his beloved wife? Does that make her the "victim" of verbal abuse? No, not necessarily.

It is almost a fad to be labeled a victim now. It's becoming easier and easier for people to seek to identify with actual victims of horrible traumas by magnifying the petty problems in their own lives or by refusing to accept responsibility for their own actions. While this might help those who are seeking to relate to victims, it is absolutely disrespectful to those who have suffered genuine trauma or abuse. Those are the true victims.

But in discussing what makes someone a real victim, we must not forget the ultimate victim and ultimate abuse—Christ and His victimization on the cross on behalf of fallen humanity.

If a victim thinks her life is bad right now, help her to think about what Jesus suffered through so she could have life—eternal life. He was beaten multiple times, mocked, spat upon, scourged, hung completely naked on a cross at a busy intersection for all the passers-by to see—and that's only *part* of His sufferings. His mental anguish was so great it caused Him to sweat drops of blood. And why did He do it? Why did the Son of God, the One who could have saved Himself and slain every one of His tormenters, allow Himself to be treated that way and murdered? He did it for each of us, victim or not, because He loves us.

No one has suffered more abuse than Christ suffered on our behalf. We are called to be partakers of Christ's suffering, as we trust in Him and are surrounded by His love and care. We should encourage victims to set aside self-pity and look to the cross, where Jesus died for all our sins. We cannot allow ourselves, or our counselees, to wallow in self-pity (which is a sin) and victimization, becoming so comfortable in it that they (or even we) don't want to be made well.

I stand firm in my belief that the power of God, working in the human life, is the *only* means by which one can heal from abuse of any kind. Only God can bring about true emotional, spiritual, and physical well-being (2 Corinthians 12:9).

Chapter One • Bible Study

Who Was the Ultimate Victim?

As you read and ponder these questions, ask yourself how Christ is able to understand your feelings and give you comfort in light of the abuse He suffered.

1. Have you been rejected?

   ____

   Isaiah 53:3: "*He is despised and rejected of men; a man of sorrows, and acquainted with grief: and we hid as it were our faces from him; he was despised, and we esteemed him not.*" (See also Mark 8:31 and Luke 17:25.)

2. Have you been degraded or humiliated?

   ____

   Matthew 27:30–31: "*And they spit upon him, and took the reed, and smote him on the head. And after that they had mocked him, they took the robe off from him, and put his own raiment on him, and led him away to crucify him.*" (I suggest reading the entire chapter of Matthew 27.)

3. Have you been shamed?

   ____

Matthew 27:28: "*And they stripped him, and put on him a scarlet robe.*" (For victims of rape, incest, and other sexual abuse, it helps knowing that Christ also suffered and overcame such indignity when He was stripped and hung naked on the Cross for their sake.)

4. Have you suffered for another's sake?

___

Philippians 1:29: "*For unto you it is given in the behalf of Christ, not only to believe on him, but also to suffer for his sake.*" And Galatians 6:2: "*Bear ye one another's burdens, and so fulfil the law of Christ.*"

5. Are you willing to allow God to help you?

___

Psalm 40:17: "*But I am poor and needy; yet the Lord thinketh upon me: thou art my help and my deliverer; make no tarrying, O my God.*" And Psalm 42:5: "*Why art thou cast down, O my soul? and why art thou disquieted in me? hope thou in God: for I shall yet praise him for the help of his countenance.*"

Write your thoughts and feelings at this time:

___

___

___

___

Chapter Two

Recalling the Past

Now a few years older, and broken by life's cruelty, she enters counseling. She desires to be made whole, to be free of the pain she feels with every breath. The counselor encourages her to recall exactly what happened in her past, to dredge up all the details, to feel the painful experience all over again. All she really wants to do is forget the past and find hope for a future. She questions, "Is remembering the past really key to my healing?" She prays for God to show her the answers, to bring all the abuse to her mind if He wants her to remember it, yet the complete memories never come. She wonders if it means she cannot heal. Yet God in His mercy ultimately brings full and complete healing, abundant grace, and courage to live, even without all the memories of the painful past.

Is it really important to remember all the painful details of our past? When we turn to the Bible for answers we might find statements that appear to be contradictory at first glance; however, it is important to look at the full meaning of each passage in context. In Isaiah 43:18 we read, "*Remember ye not the former things, neither consider the things of old.*" Yet in Isaiah 46:9 it says, "*Remember the former things of old.*" What is God trying to tell us? God wants us to forget the bad things. Forget our sins and slipups, failures and foibles. If we've confessed our sins, He's forgiven us for them. Time to move on and leave those sinful behaviors and thoughts behind. He wants us to forget who we used to be and focus on who He wants us to be in Him. Conversely, He wants us to remember what He has done for us. He wants us to recall the ways He has led us in the past and trust He will do so in the future. Just like it says in Jeremiah 6:16, "*Thus saith the Lord, Stand ye in the ways, and see, and ask for the old paths, where is the good way, and walk therein, and ye shall find rest for your souls.*"

In recent decades there has been much ado about false memory syndrome and repressed memories. Many of these so-called memories that have surfaced in counseling have been proven to be fabricated. In fact, many times a counselee has been walked through the process of guided imagery or hypnosis (things Christians should not be involved in at all), often without even being aware of the fact, before being able to "recall" a supposed memory of abuse from her past. A counselor should not directly encourage a victim to try to recall past abuse that is not currently remembered, but to look forward to the life ahead of her. While there are times for reflection, and certain memories may be necessary to recall, we must avoid falling into the trap of "yesteryear."

It would never be appropriate to use memories as a way to exaggerate past events, to shift blame, to excuse bad behavior, avoid responsibility, cling to unforgiveness, blame God, or live in fear.

It would be appropriate to reflect on the past to help us understand established patterns of thinking and behavior; to understand who we need to seek forgiveness from; who we need to forgive; to confess our sin; to establish new patterns of thinking and behavior (Ephesians 4:22–24); and to press on to the future, unhindered by the past (Hebrews 12:1, 2).

In her book *Manufacturing Victims: What the Psychology Industry is Doing to People*[3], Dr. Dineen discusses the fabrication and "psychologizing" of victims and states that it involves the practice of constructing a theory about victimization; applying that theory to an individual; turning personal events into psychological symbols, which are then expressed in psychological language; and creating a need for psychologists who can interpret the symbols and cure the patient.

I simply wish to clarify that it is the gospel—the Word of God—that sets the captive free and binds up the heart of the brokenhearted. There is no need for all these unfounded, unscientific psychological labels (Isaiah 61). Our focus, as counselors, should be to reveal the heart of the victim, enable her to focus on God and His providence, and facilitate the development of a genuine relationship between her and Jesus.

The key? A victim must *desire* to be made whole (John 5:6). Without that desire, it won't matter what technique or methodology is used, biblical or psychological, there will never be healing. In Christ alone is found true healing. In Christ, a true *victim* can become a true *victor*. First Corinthians 15:57 promises, "*But thanks be to God, which giveth us the victory through our Lord Jesus Christ.*" By faith we can grasp hold of His promises and look forward to the abundant life that God wants us to experience. "*For whatsoever is born of God overcometh the world: and this is the victory that overcometh the world, even our faith*" (1 John 5:4).

Chapter Two • Bible Study

What to Do with the Past

As you review these texts, write down what the Bible says you should do about the past.

Hebrews 12:1–2: "*Wherefore seeing we also are compassed about with so great a cloud of witnesses, let us lay aside every weight, and the sin which doth so easily beset us, and let us run with patience the race that is set before us, Looking unto Jesus the author and finisher of our faith; who for the joy that was set before him endured the cross, despising the shame, and is set down at the right hand of the throne of God.*"

____

____

____

____

Ephesians 4:22–24: "*That ye put off concerning the former conversation the old man, which is corrupt according to the deceitful lusts; And be renewed in the spirit of your mind; And that ye put on the new man, which after God is created in righteousness and true holiness."*

Isaiah 43:18: "*Remember ye not the former things, neither consider the things of old.*"

Philippians 3:13–14: "*Brethren, I count not myself to have apprehended: but this one thing I do, forgetting those things which are behind, and reaching forth unto those things which are before, I press toward the mark for the prize of the high calling of God in Christ Jesus.*"

CHAPTER THREE

WHO IS RESPONSIBLE?

"It must have been my fault. I deserve to be treated this way," she thinks, contemplating the recent behavior of her abusive boyfriend. Struggling to know what God would have her do, she pleads in desperation for Him to help her. As He leads her out of the abusive relationship and into a deeper walk with Him, He reveals to her what was her responsibility and what was not.

I have the utmost compassion and empathy for those who have been abused, whether suffering at the hands of a violent father or mother, being the recipient of unwanted sexual advances and contact, having nightmares from childhood incest or rape, or even experiencing something as horrific as war. All these situations have the potential to cause trauma, and it is difficult to heal from trauma.

People who have experienced these types of situations are true victims. They need to find hope and healing.

I know from my own experience that I can't, and don't, have peace when I continue to remain a victim (versus seeking to overcome the pain and live a productive life); when I refuse to allow God to bring about change in my life or when I refuse to let God take care of the person who has hurt me in His own way and time. I can trust the Lord to make things right. He encourages me in Romans 12:19 when He says, "*Dearly beloved, avenge not yourselves, but rather give place unto wrath: for it is written, Vengeance is mine; I will repay, saith the Lord.*"

A victim must come to the point where she clearly understands that while she may not have been responsible for what happened to her (rape, molestation as a child, etc.), she is responsible for her subsequent response to what has happened (1 Corinthians 10:13).

Does she harbor resentment and hatred toward the abuser? Does she become promiscuous? Does she now abuse her own children? Does she use the past abuse or trauma as an excuse for her current unacceptable behavior (*e.g.*, drug or alcohol use and other forms of self-destructive behavior)? All these instances, and more, abound.

Unfortunately, humanistic psychology too often allows the victim to believe these responses are appropriate because of what has happened in the past. "*You can't help the way you feel; you were abused.*" "*Your family was dysfunctional.*" And on it goes. Can we honestly name one family, since the fall of Adam, which has not been dysfunctional? I don't think so.

In an effort to presumably protect the victim, psychologists often tell victims to "set boundaries." Unfortunately, this often creates selfishness and, as we all know, selfishness is a sin. While there are certainly proper and ethical boundaries (maintaining privacy and confidentiality in personal relationships and taking time for family and loved ones, for rejuvenation, and the study of God's Word) that must be established in all relationships, as Christians we are not to let our conduct be the same as the conduct of those who are not in Christ. We have a new heart, a new nature, given to us by God. Ezekiel 36:26 says, "*A new heart also will I give you, and a new spirit will I put within you.*" We are not to draw an imaginary line around ourselves and prohibit others from encroaching on our "space" just because we may not want to inconvenience ourselves or feel any pain.

What if Christ had set "boundaries" such as these? Surely He would never have given His life for you or me. Wouldn't that have been a tragedy? I for one am thankful that Christ chose to give His all that I might inherit eternal life through Him.

We are not to focus on "self," but on God. In more grievous instances of victimization (such as physical, emotional, or sexual abuse), we, through prayer and God's grace, must still find forgiveness (which is a gift from God) for the perpetrator and allow God to heal the wounds. God alone is able to forgive sin, and He alone is able to impart to us the forgiveness we need for those who have hurt us (Daniel 9:9: "*To the Lord our God belong mercies and forgivenesses, though we have rebelled against him*").

It is important to note, however, that *forgiveness does not necessarily mean reconciliation. There are consequences to all of our actions.* Sometimes a family member who has abused other family members may be forgiven, but not reconciled. This may be considered a proper type of "boundary."

What would this proper boundary look like? Take for example the grandfather (or uncle or brother-in-law or mother, etc.) who molests his granddaughter. When his daughter, the mother of the victim, finds out, what should she do? She should take immediate steps to protect her daughter. More than likely, the mother will wish to keep her daughter from her grandfather from that point forward. This is not in itself a sign of unforgiveness. This may be considered setting proper boundaries, and it is the consequences of one's actions.

Granted, forgiveness may not, and probably should not, come immediately, but when it does come it does not mean that the mother, daughter, and grandfather all live happily ever after, enjoying one another's company at all family get-togethers.

Victims need to learn to accept responsibility for their own subsequent actions as adults (*e.g.*, lying, stealing, committing adultery, perpetrating abuse upon another, etc.), without negating the responsibility of the actual abuser. Many have a difficult time comprehending how they can accept responsibility for their own actions without diminishing the abuser's responsibility. It's important to remember that we each have accountability to God for our thoughts, words, and deeds. Taking responsibility for our own sinful actions and reactions doesn't minimize an abuser's responsibility to us or to God.

We also need to learn to set aside petty sensitivities and to overlook another's tactless or insensitive comments at times. I'm not talking about grievous crimes or actual abuses here, only the harboring of resentment toward someone who may have said or done something, perhaps even inadvertently, that may have caused the "victim" to feel hurt. When someone says something hurtful it should be addressed and forgotten. If it cannot be addressed, then the one who is offended has the opportunity to take it to Christ, to leave it at the cross, and to forgive the other person. No one suffered more verbal, emotional, spiritual, or physical abuse than Christ did on our behalf. Yet while hanging on the cross, He prayed, "*Father, forgive them; for they know not what they do.*" Should we really complain or be unforgiving?

Chapter Three • Bible Study

Who Is Responsible?

Be honest as you search your heart for the answers to the following questions.

1. Have you harbored hatred or resentment toward someone who has abused you? (Galatians 5:19–21: *"Now the works of the flesh are manifest, which are these; adultery, fornication, uncleanness, lasciviousness, idolatry, witchcraft, hatred, variance, emulations, wrath, strife, seditions, heresies, envyings, murders, drunkenness, revellings, and such like: of the which I tell you before, as I have also told you in time past, that they which do such things shall not inherit the kingdom of God.")*

____

____

____

____

2. Are you willing to accept responsibility for your own sinful actions or reactions, rather than blaming them on your parents, your upbringing, your

past abuse, etc.? (1 Corinthians 10:13: "*There hath no temptation taken you but such as is common to man: but God is faithful, who will not suffer you to be tempted above that ye are able; but will with the temptation also make a way to escape, that ye may be able to bear it.*")

____

____

____

____

3. Are you willing to extend forgiveness to those who have hurt you? Even if you feel they don't "deserve" it? (Ephesians 4:32: "*And be ye kind one to another, tenderhearted, forgiving one another, even as God for Christ's sake hath forgiven you.*" And Matthew 6 14: "*For if ye forgive men their trespasses, your heavenly Father will also forgive you: But if ye forgive not men their trespasses, neither will your Father forgive your trespasses.*")

____

____

____

____

Chapter Four

A New Heart = A New Life

Thoughts of suicide filled her mind as she focused on all the injustices she had experienced in her life. "Why was life so hard?" she pondered. As the depression took root ever deeper in her mind, her thoughts became more and more centered on her problems and the only way she thought she could get out of them—suicide. Satan had so deceived her that she believed killing herself would be a blessing to those around her, that somehow they would be better off without her.

This might seem like a strange topic to bring up when discussing abuse victims and their possible thoughts of suicide; however, the way I see it, no one can heal without having a new heart and a new purpose for living. That being the case, how do we go about receiving a new heart, new thoughts, and actions?

We need to study God's Word, pray daily (Psalm 51:10 is a good place to start), and seek to have a close relationship with Christ. It is through this relationship that we will be recreated into His likeness and the pain of the past will dissipate in the light of His love. It is by beholding Him that we become changed into His likeness. (See 2 Corinthians 3:18.)

While working with individuals who have been abused, I have learned to distinguish between those who are seeking truth and healing from those who are simply seeking sympathy and an excuse to live as they please. Those who are genuinely seeking truth and healing have a much greater measure of peace and joy amidst undesirable circumstances, and have a greater and more complete recovery through Christ.

God's Word has promised each of us a new heart (Ezekiel 36:25–28) and tells us to keep our hearts with all diligence (Proverbs 4:23). As children of God, we are responsible for the continued nurturing of the heart in order to mature in Christ.

There are three indicators of that which resides in the heart—behavior (acting out, committing crimes, etc.); feelings (self-pity, resentment, anger, etc.); and attitudes (prideful, negative, etc.). Each of these areas must be addressed when working with a victim who truly desires to be made whole.

As counselors, we must address things at the heart level with those who come to us for help. We must ask them hard questions: "*Do you really want answers?*" "*Are you willing to listen to what God has to say and to do what He says?*" The main reasons counselees are not helped are because (a) they don't want to be; (b) they don't know the Word of God very well or what the answers are; and (c) when they realize that God expects something of them (perhaps a change of lifestyle or attitude), that they actually have a responsibility (to surrender to God), they simply don't want it.

A good way to get to the heart of the matter, to root out the idols of the heart so to speak, is to ask questions such as, "*What do you think about most often?*" "*What's been most on your mind in the past week?*" The answers may surprise you, but they will undoubtedly give you insight to the counselee's idols and heart condition. ("Idols" simply meaning whatever is taking the place of God in the person's life.)

For instance, if a counselee (victim) says that thoughts of past abuse or suicide are prominent, then you will know that there is a strong focus on self rather than on God. From this point forward, once you have discussed these painful topics and made certain she is safe, you should work with her to put the idols of her heart to death (Romans 8:13) and to develop in her a relationship with God and a character suited for His Kingdom. All of us can work on changing our thoughts and actions. By God's grace we can overcome every challenge. In 1 John 4:4 we're taught, "*Ye are of God, little children, and have overcome them: because greater is he that is in you, than he that is in the world.*"

The Bible says we are each responsible for our own actions, thoughts, words, and feelings. If they are sinful, we are responsible for confessing those sins and seeking forgiveness. Victims need to understand that their (sometimes) obsessive thoughts of past trauma can actually be sinful, and they need to establish new patterns of thinking and behavior (Ephesians 4:22–24;

1 Peter 1:22). Victims need to learn to look to God. He loves them. He has compassion for them. He has felt their pain. He desires to bring them healing and wholeness, to change them from victim status to victorious overcomer through the power of the Holy Spirit (1 Corinthians 15:56–58 and 1 John 5:4).

One look at the sufferings of Christ and His apostles should encourage us. It should help us see that we are not the first to suffer, nor have we suffered alone or in vain, and our sufferings (always) fade in comparison with what our dear Savior suffered. He did it all for us. Is there a way we can turn our sorrow into joy and bring glory to our Lord? Yes, there is! By allowing God to heal us, we can share our testimony with others and encourage them. More on that ahead.

Chapter Four • Bible Study

A New Heart = A New Life

As you review the following Scriptures, write down what the text means to you and how you can apply it to your life today.

Ezekiel 36:26–27: "*A new heart also will I give you, and a new spirit will I put within you: and I will take away the stony heart out of your flesh, and I will give you an heart of flesh. And I will put my spirit within you, and cause you to walk in my statutes, and ye shall keep my judgments, and do them.*"

____

____

____

____

Proverbs 4:23: "*Keep thy heart with all diligence; for out of it are the issues of life.*" And Proverbs 23:7: "*For as he thinketh in his heart, so is he.*"

____

____

____

Romans 8:13: "*For if ye live after the flesh, ye shall die: but if ye through the Spirit do mortify the deeds of the body, ye shall live.*"

1 John 5:4: "*For whatsoever is born of God overcometh the world: and this is the victory that overcometh the world, even our faith.*"

1 John 1:9: "*If we confess our sins, he is faithful and just to forgive us our sins, and to cleanse us from all unrighteousness.*"

Chapter Five

Suffering: What's the Point?

"Why me, Lord?" she cried out through her tears. She couldn't understand why God had allowed so much suffering in her life. "Why did I have to be abused, raped, beaten?" "What's wrong with me?" "Do you even care, God?" "What's the purpose in life?" "Why must I go through all of this?" "Is there no end to the pain?" She buried her head in her hands and waited for some kind of answer, for something to begin to make sense in her confused and tortured mind.

One of the most frequently asked questions is, "*Why did this happen to me*?" or "*Why do people suffer*?" It is often difficult to comprehend, even though the answer may sound simplistic. We suffer because we live in a sinful world. We are sinful beings with a sinful nature. Then the question becomes, "*Why do Christians suffer*?" The answer is the same, although there is more to it for the Christian. *For the Christian, there is victory in Christ.*

Life is hard because we live in a world of sin, a world where people are more concerned about themselves than God or others. God allows the trials in life for our benefit—although it hardly ever seems like a benefit at the time. It is through the trials of life, however, that we are brought into closer connection with our Savior and, if we cling to Him, He will perfect His character within us. We need to take a look at how a Christian obtains victory through Christ, and we'll do that by finding out what justification and sanctification mean in the life of a Christian, victim or not.

In 1 Corinthians 6:11 ("*ye are sanctified, but ye are justified in the name of the Lord Jesus, and by the Spirit of our God*"), we learn that we are justified and sanctified through the Lord Jesus and the Holy Spirit. But just what does justification mean? It is a legal declaration that man is no longer held accountable for his sin. He is seen, through Christ's sacrifice, as righteous. Justification is God's work alone. It is a one-time work by God. This means victims and abusers alike can come to God, seek His forgiveness, and rest assured that He has forgiven them for their sins; providing, of course, that the repentance is genuine and the individual has a sincere desire to do what is right and the corresponding actions. Justification is vindication.

Sanctification, however, is the work of a lifetime. It is an internal heart condition. It is the process of turning from sin, and turning toward Christ, so we can become more like Jesus. It is a continuous work, in cooperation with God, throughout our lives. In 1 John 1:10 we learn that *"[if] we say that we have not sinned, we make him a liar, and his word is not in us."* Having sinned, however, does not mean we are to continue in sin, for the Bible also instructs us to *"[be] ye therefore perfect, even as your Father which is in heaven is perfect"* (Matthew 5:48).

So how do we address the question that often arises when discussing sin—the question of the *"sins of the father"* (Exodus 20:5–6)? It is true that tendencies toward certain sins, as well as character defects and genetic imperfections, are passed from parents to children from one generation to another, but as Christians we are given a new nature in Christ; the grace to have the opportunity to live according to God's Word. We are not "doomed" or "predestined" to live in sin because we (or our parents) have been sinning or have been sinned against. We each have the blessed hope of new life through Christ Jesus. We will cover this topic in more detail in a later chapter.

As counselors, we must be empathetic. We must show victims mercy and grace, but never give them an excuse to remain in sin (*e.g.*, a disease label, shifting blame, etc.). We must show them that God has given them victory already, through His power, if they will only choose to accept it. Texts such as 1 Corinthians 15:57; 1 John 4:20–21; 1 John 5:1–5; 2 Corinthians 5:17, 20–21; and 1 Corinthians 6:9–11 are helpful in pointing victims in the right direction.

From these texts we learn that there are two kinds of suffering: suffering that is productive and suffering that is not. Suffering is also designed as a tool to bring people to repentance. For the non-Christian, however, suffering will not produce anything good of an eternal (everlasting) consequence. However, for the Christian,

God intends to use suffering for our own good and for His glory (1 Peter 4:12–19).

Some would ask, "*Why me*?" but the question is really, "*Why* not *you*?" God doesn't owe any of us anything. He never promised a life without trials. In fact, He said quite the opposite in John 16:33: "*These things I have spoken unto you, that in me ye might have peace. In the world ye shall have tribulation: but be of good cheer; I have overcome the world.*" Jesus told us we would experience trials and troubles, but He offered the reassurance that He has overcome the world and, through Him, we may overcome all trials. God created us for His pleasure, for us to serve and worship Him. Christ suffered more than we ever will. In fact, we can't even imagine the depth of His suffering and shame. Now some may think there have been more horrendous crimes than what Christ suffered, and indeed there have been very gruesome crimes perpetrated upon others. The difference lies in this simple fact: We don't have the power to do something about abuse and to avenge ourselves at all times. Think about this for a moment: I believe one of the greatest temptations Christ had was to *not* do something when He was tortured and abused for our sake. We have no choice ... we are powerless at times to defend ourselves. But Christ had all power in heaven and earth, and He did not do anything for the very purpose of fulfilling His part of the great plan of redemption. Now, *that's* a trial!

Getting back to the passages mentioned above, in 1 Peter 4 there are four key points that should be noted. We should:

1. Rejoice in the cause of Christ (verses 12–13);
2. Glorify God (verse 14);
3. Be righteous, suffer for righteousness (verses 16–18);
4. Trust God and do good (verse 19).

It is essential to understand that salvation is by grace (unmerited favor) and that we do not deserve anything of the Lord. All is freely bestowed upon us in His loving mercy. Do any of us truly have any merit with God on our own? No. We can thank Jesus for His work on our behalf.

There are several important points to understand about suffering. God trains us through suffering (Hebrews 12). Suffering is the result of a fallen world (Genesis 3). God is in control of this fallen world (Psalm 19). Suffering is not beyond God's control (Job and 1 Peter). God's purpose is often a secret to man (Deuteronomy 29:29). Often there is pain without immediate answers, but God is always there (Psalm 42 and 43). And God is always worthy of our endurance (Hebrews 12:3–7). If we could keep this in mind at all times we'd be less likely to question and become discouraged when we experience painful trials.

In order for any of our answers to make sense, the victim must first be firmly established in Christ. She must understand we are all in a cosmic battle; we are at war. Satan is battling against Christ for the control of this world and its inhabitants. We are the pawns he uses to hurt Christ. When Satan succeeds in hurting one of God's children, God is hurt. He loves you and me *that* much. Therefore, the little things we do (*e.g.*, pray, read Scripture, forgive others, go to church, etc.) are all very critical. God is glorified as we walk with Him. We must also understand that *pain is for a little while.* It will not last forever. There is hope for something better in life—in this life and in eternal life.

When we see God as He really is, all pain and suffering will be inconsequential. He is omnipotent, all-powerful, and He loves us so much He gave His only Son that we might have life as we follow Him. No matter how we may feel, we need to continue to do good even in the midst of pain and suffering (Phil. 3:12–14; 1 Peter 4:19).

We must also understand that we have a responsibility to repent of our own wrong actions and to seek forgiveness from others when necessary. We must do what is right—what God requires of us—at each step (Hebrews 12:15–17). As we grow in Christ and Christian maturity, we will see that victimization actually helps increase our view of God and who He is. When we step back from the pain to recall how God has led, protected, and walked with us "through the water" in the past (no matter how bad things were, they could have been even worse), our faith will increase and we'll be assured that whatever trial we have experienced, or are experiencing, is not in vain. As one writer explains, God does everything in His power to rescue each of us:

> *"Thank God, He has presented to our imagination no picture of a sorrowful shepherd return-*

ing without the sheep. The parable does not speak of failure but of success and joy in the recovery. Here is the divine guarantee that not even one of the straying sheep of God's fold is overlooked, not one is left unsuccored. Every one that will submit to be ransomed, Christ will rescue from the pit of corruption and from the briers of sin.

"Desponding soul, take courage, even though you have done wickedly. Do not think that perhaps God will pardon your transgressions and permit you to come into His presence. God has made the first advance. While you were in rebellion against Him, He went forth to seek you. With the tender heart of the shepherd He left the ninety and nine and went out into the wilderness to find that which was lost. The soul, bruised and wounded and ready to perish, He encircles in His arms of love and joyfully bears it to the fold of safety."[4]

What a beautiful picture of Christ's love for us! To know that whatever our circumstances or situation may be, there is a Savior present, ready to care for and heal the wounds! However, don't overlook the part we have to do—*submit*. We must submit to Christ to be ransomed.

Along with this beautiful picture of the Shepherd is a story told by Edith Schaeffer in her book *Affliction.*[5] She talks about the shepherd who must break his lamb's leg, splint it, and then carry the lamb to keep it from running away and getting hurt. The pain is very real—to the lamb and to the shepherd who must hurt his precious lamb—but the love that grows out of the pain is everlasting. As the lamb heals and can walk on its own again, it will never leave the side of the shepherd it loves.

What a precious example of the love God has for us! It is very painful for God to allow bad things to happen to us. It is painful for Him to watch us suffer. But He alone knows what's best for us and what will keep us close to Him so we will ultimately gain eternal life (Isaiah 57).

Schaeffer goes on to recommend that we pose the following question to the victim, "*What are the possibilities*?" Now think about that for a moment before you continue. What *are* the possibilities? Suggested answers: *Jesus may come tomorrow. I may die tomorrow. The person who hurt me may die tomorrow. The situation may change entirely—through me, through the person who hurt me, or through circumstances. Or nothing may change.*

As we ponder these possibilities, it is important to make sure we understand God's sovereignty, goodness, and providence. Let's address these one by one in the next chapter.

Chapter Five • Bible Study

What's the Purpose of Suffering?

Read Job 3 and 1 Peter 1, then look up the following verses in your Bible and write out the meaning of each in your own words. How does this exercise help you to understand suffering?

1 Peter 4:12–19:

____

____

____

____

____

____

Deuteronomy 29:29:

____

____

____

____

____

____

Romans 8:28:

1 Peter 2:20–21; 4:16, 19:

Revelation 2:10:

Chapter Six

Understanding the Attributes of God

In her anger, she denied that God was with her, watching over her and protecting her. She failed to see how He could have loved her and yet allowed all those horrible experiences to occur in her life. It didn't make sense. As she prayed for Him to help her understand, the Holy Spirit comforted her and directed her to the promises in God's Word and her need to believe them and trust in her Lord and Savior. "Surely, He who made the heavens and the earth, He who maintains everything at every moment, must have had His eye on me and carried me through according to His plan and purpose," she finally realized.

God has many attributes, including sovereignty, goodness, and providence. For victims to learn to trust God and to accept what has happened in their lives and move forward in faith, it is important to have a better understanding of these peculiar attributes of God. Let's begin with God's sovereignty.

Sovereignty is an incommunicable attribute of God whereby He does whatever He pleases. His omnipotence means He has the power to carry out His will, whatever it may be. God's will is holy; it is not arbitrary, demanding, or exacting. His will is not for our destruction, but for our salvation; therefore, whatever His will is, we can rest assured that it is for our best good.

There are several texts that will help us to come to a deeper understanding of God's sovereignty, and these include: Jeremiah 32:17; Matthew 19:26; 2 Samuel 7:28; 2 Kings 19:15; Job 41:11; Psalm 24:1, 10; Psalm 115:3; Psalm 135:6; Isaiah 61:1; John 19:11; Romans 14:11; and Ephesians 1:11.

Now let's talk about goodness. Goodness is a communicable attribute of God. God is the final standard of good, and all He is and does is worthy of approval. Good is defined by God and by His character and what He decrees (Luke 18:19; Psalm 100:5; Psalm 106:1; Exodus 33:19; Nahum 1:7; Mark 10:18; James 1:5, 17; Lamentations 3:25 and 2 Peter 1:3).

Out of His goodness, God calls His children to Him. Knowing that He is all good, we can then believe (and trust) that everything He brings into our lives, or allows to happen to us, is for our good and for our best interest, as well as for His own glory. Since God is perfectly sovereign, He alone has the power to allow things to happen in our lives or to keep things from happening in our lives. So when a victim asks the question, "*Why did God let this happen*?" we should not be ashamed to answer that God *could* have stopped it, but He *didn't*. The reason He chose not to stop it is known often only to Him. It should comfort us to know that God weighs everything in the balance, knowing what the outcome will be, and He allows certain things to occur to refine and fit us for heaven.

God's decrees and providence are defined as the eternal plans of God—plans that were laid before the creation of the world. There is preservation—God is continually involved with all created things in such a way that He keeps them existing. He maintains the properties with which He created them (Hebrews 1:3; Colossians 1:17; Nehemiah 9:6). There is concurrence—He cooperates with all created things in every action, directing their distinctive properties to cause them to act as they do (Ephesians 1:11). And there's governance—He directs them to fulfill His purposes (Psalm 103:19; Daniel 4:35; Romans 11:36; Romans 8:28).

The key point for us to understand is nothing happens to us outside of God's will and knowledge. God is fully aware of what we are doing and what is happening to us at all times. He sees all. He knows all. In the book *Behind a Frowning Providence*[6], John J. Murray states, "*God's plan is: perfect, exhaustive, for our ultimate good, and secret.*" The doctrine of providence teaches us we are still responsible for our actions and that our actions have real results and change the course of events. We learn prayer is a specific kind of action that has definite results and changes the course of events (John 16:24). We also learn that we must act.

To answer the question, "*Where was God*?": He was there with you and was working in accord with what is best for you, for His glory, and for His Kingdom. We need to learn to measure God's love by His promises, not by His providence. Will you trust God?

Chapter Six • Bible Study

Understanding the Attributes of God

It's difficult to understand God's perfect character at times, especially when we observe sin and suffering in our own lives. Truly, we can never fully understand His character. As you review the following texts, write what each one means to you and how you can know God better and trust Him more fully because of it.

Jeremiah 32:17: "*Ah Lord GOD! behold, thou hast made the heaven and the earth by thy great power and stretched out arm, and there is nothing too hard for thee.*"

____

____

____

____

Psalm 100:5: "*For the Lord is good; his mercy is everlasting; and his truth endureth to all generations.*"

____

____

Colossians 1:17: "*And he is before all things, and by him all things consist.*"

Genesis 50:20: "*But as for you, ye thought evil against me; but God meant it unto good, to bring to pass, as it is this day, to save much people alive.*"

Jeremiah 29:11: "*For I know the thoughts that I think toward you, saith the* Lord*, thoughts of peace, and not of evil, to give you an expected end.*"

Chapter Seven

Love God, Love Your Neighbor—Not Yourself

She struggled with her identity and worth. "Who am I?" she would ask herself. Oh, she'd heard about how she was supposed to love herself and see herself as someone very valuable, but how could she? She didn't feel valuable or lovable. She felt worthless. "What gives my life meaning? What makes me worth something? How could anyone love me?" she questioned.

Now, we all know God intends for us to keep all ten of His commandments. They can be summed up in what the Bible tells us are the two great commandments: to love God and to love our neighbor. Nowhere does it mention the need to love "self" (Mark 12:29–31). There is an assumption in this command that we already love ourselves and, if we would love our neighbors and God as much as we love ourselves, we would fulfill the purpose of God in our lives. Why, then, does the world insist on making it "all about me"? (As in, "you need to love yourself," "you can't love others if you don't love yourself.") The truth is, it is *all about God*. It's about

His mercy, His love, His sacrifice, and His plan for our lives.

When we continually focus on the impact of what someone has said or done to us, we become too self-involved. The focus is on self, not on God.

There are many negative aspects of this self-esteem movement. Some of them include the fact that the movement itself is counter-productive and most often ineffective; it makes us self-centered, and it tends to give license to (or promote) sin. How can we truly love, encourage, and comfort one another if we are continually focused on ourselves? If we focus solely on our own thoughts, goals, activities, etc., will it not lead us to sin? Will we not eventually turn our hobbies, recreational pursuits, or entertainment into idols? Idolatry—whether the worship of self, something, or someone else—is sin. To know and love God is the supreme goal in life. To know who we are in Christ is the ultimate "self-esteem." We are to measure our self-worth by the price Christ paid for our ransom. It was a higher price than any of us can even imagine!

So where does our identity come from? How do we receive esteem? As counselors, we should point our counselees to God's Word—the only authority and sufficiency for our every need. Our esteem, our identity, comes from knowing we are children of the Most High King. God esteems us (Isaiah 66:1–2) and our main concern should be "*How does God see me*?" not "*How do I feel about myself*?"

Sometimes victims feel so much shame they can't believe God will accept them as they are at any given moment. They think they need to do something to earn God's favor. But Romans 8:1 assures us, "*There is therefore now no condemnation to them which are in Christ Jesus, who walk not after the flesh, but after the Spirit.*" That is something to rejoice about! God loves us just as we are. Fortunately, when we come in contact with God, He doesn't leave us as we are. He changes us, and always for the better.

When we continue in self-hatred and self-condemnation, it is often because we want the attention "victim" status gives us; we don't want to live the way God has called us to live; or we don't want to accept the fact that by accepting Christ (fully), we must change. (See Romans 12:1–3.)

A key question to ask victims who insist on remaining such is, "*Why do you let this event that happened (or this person that hurt you) so long ago continue to shape and define who you are today*?" It is a question each person who truly wants to heal will need to carefully consider and ponder. There is no glory or honor in remaining a victim. Rather, we are fulfilled and uplifted as we seek to overcome all prior trauma and dire circumstances and to live a life pleasing to God.

We need to love God. And in loving God supremely, we will learn to love our neighbor as God intends. How do we learn to love God? The same way we learn to love anyone else—by spending time with Him. We begin to understand God better when we read His Word (the

Bible), when we pray, when we obey His commands, and when we allow His Holy Spirit to transform our lives.

Once we do that, the natural result of a loving relationship with the Lord is love toward others. We will find ourselves more compassionate, eager to serve others, and help those in need. We will no longer be self-focused, but God and "others"-focused.

A key point to remember is that self-esteem ("self" in any form) is at the heart of our rebellion against God and, therefore, can never be part of the solution. Again, it's all about God, not all about us.

CHAPTER SEVEN • BIBLE STUDY

LOVE GOD, LOVE YOUR NEIGHBOR—NOT YOURSELF

Can you think of some of the dangers involved in being self-focused rather than God-focused? Compare the following statements with the Scripture texts given. Do you see how being self-focused changes our thinking and draws us away from God rather than to Him?

Statement:

"*You must love yourself before you can love others.*"

Scripture:

Matthew 22:39; Galatians 5:14; John 15:12–13; 1 John 4:7–8

Compare:

____

____

____

____

Statement:

"*You need to think positive about yourself in order to accomplish anything good.*"

Scripture:

Psalm 8:4; John 15:4–5; Ephesians 2:4–7; Philippians 3:7–14

Compare:

____

____

____

____

Statement:

"*You have to forgive yourself before you can have peace or forgive others.*"

Scripture:

Daniel 9:9; John 16:33; 1 Corinthians 1:18–21; Colossians 2:8–14

Compare:

____

____

____

____

Chapter Eight

Change is Necessary

"How can I bear this guilt and shame any longer?" her head screamed at her. She thought about all the mistakes she had made and all the bad things that had happened to her, and she believed she must have been to blame. "I don't want to live like this anymore," she determined. In her mind there was a glimmer of hope that her life could change. "But how?" she questioned.

One of my favorite texts for sharing with victims is Psalm 25:20–21, where it says, "*O keep my soul, and deliver me: let me not be ashamed; for I put my trust in thee. Let integrity and uprightness preserve me; for I wait on thee.*" If we trust in the Lord to refine and shape our characters, if we allow Him to be the Lord of our lives, we need never be ashamed.

Everyone at some time or another has to change things, whether they are sinful thoughts or sinful habits. The focus should be on changing our thinking and our behavior so that we are in conformity to Christ's likeness.

Several key texts in the Bible talk about change, and some of them include: Romans 12, beginning with verse 2; John 16:7 and on; Proverbs 3:3, 5; and many others. It is by the power of the Holy Spirit that we are able to make changes in our lives. The Holy Spirit works within us in an orderly way. He is a genuine being, a person, and a member of the Godhead (Father, Son, and Holy Spirit). A relationship with the Holy Spirit will bring change to our hearts and, therefore, our lives. Change is painful but necessary. There is no choice. Change, for the better or for the worse, occurs whether we want it to or not, and lasting change—the sanctification that brings about salvation through Christ—can't be accomplished without the assistance of the Holy Spirit.

The larger context of change consists of becoming involved with others and church (*e.g.*, worship, baptism, outreach, Communion, etc.). A checklist for change could possibly look something like this:

1. Have the right attitude and commit to Christ.
2. Identify the problem or problems.
3. Find scriptural support.
4. Pray.
5. Have accountability.
6. Come up with a plan to achieve the goal of change.
7. Commit to the process even if you stumble.
8. Don't neglect other areas of your life.

Guilt and shame are common characteristics seen in most victims. Now, admittedly, some victims do not really want to change their "victim" status and experience healing. Change can be frightening, and perhaps this has become a security for them and they either do not want, or are afraid, to let go. It could be due to fear of change, not wanting to be accountable, or other factors.

If, however, a victim really does want to change, then it's important for her to know that freedom from guilt and shame comes from Christ. Romans 8:1 tells us, "*There is therefore now no condemnation to them which are in Christ Jesus, who walk not after the flesh, but after the Spirit.*" If she has asked herself the questions, "*Have I wronged God? Have I wronged someone else? Have I violated a standard I set for myself?*" and the answer is no, then she needs to let go of the guilt and not wrongly (falsely) condemn herself. Satan, after all, is the accuser of the brethren.

Forgiveness is a gift of God—we do not have it within ourselves to forgive ourselves. It is God's prerogative. God gives us the gift of forgiveness for others when we have been wronged, and He promises us that when we seek His forgiveness and when we are truly repentant, He will forgive us. The only thing we can do is accept, by faith, God's promise of forgiveness. He willingly forgives all who come to Him in repentance.

Psalm 51 is a beautiful illustration of admission of wrongdoing to God and the acknowledgment of God's willingness to offer us mercy, forgiveness, and grace.

The Bible doesn't tell us to "forgive ourselves." It tells us to repent and believe (Mark 1:15). First John 1:9 tells us, "*If we confess our sins, he is faithful and just to forgive us our sins, and to cleanse us from all unrighteousness.*" We may ask for forgiveness from God at any time and be assured that He will forgive our sins.

Our goal should be to help victims do the hard work of overcoming, of seeing them to the point of meeting God where He is, of turning the perpetrator over to God, and allowing God to give them a new identity and define who they are. God has been faithful all along and will continue to be faithful. The victim must learn to trust God on a new level, to serve God and to worship Him. Change isn't quick and it isn't easy. We may have lifetimes of habits and thoughts, wounds and memories, that we need to take captive and surrender to God (2 Corinthians 10:5). However, one thing is for certain—as we allow the Holy Spirit to change us into Christ's likeness, we will be made whole.

Chapter Eight • Bible Study

Change Is Necessary

Why is change necessary to overcome abuse and live a life that is pleasing to God? List the Scripture references that prove biblical change is necessary.

____

____

____

____

Read Psalm 51 and write, in your own words, what it means to you.

____

____

____

____

____

____

____

____

Chapter Nine

Understanding the Victim

Her greatest fears were of being unlovable and unloved. She feared rejection, disappointment, and imperfection. She feared failure and defeat. In her mind she believed others would not like her if they knew her past. She believed she had to "fix" everything for everyone and be everything to everyone. It was an impossible goal. The breakthrough came when she discovered that she needed only to seek the Lord's approval and affirmation, not man's. God loved her and, once she understood that, she was free in Christ—free to confess her sins, to admit her failures, to cry about her pain, and to seek the loving reassurance that only the holy Heavenly Father can give.

In order to help those who are genuine victims or who perceive themselves as such, it is crucial to understand the thinking process of the victim and to provide biblical insight as to how she can heal from the pain and shame of the past. True healing cannot come without the acknowledgement and understanding of sin and the application of grace. So let's take a look at sin—as it may appear in the victim's life.

I have often heard people say that they are not responsible for what they do because of what happened to them in the past. "*I was molested as a child, therefore I molested my kids.*" "*I didn't know any better because that's how my parents treated me.*" The list could go on and on. But then again, I have also heard that the person is not responsible because God "*visits the sins of the father upon the children to the third and fourth generation*" (Exodus 20:5–6). If that is so, then how can we be responsible for our sins if God made us to sin by cursing us? It is also good to point out that, in the above-referenced verse, the last part, "*of them that hate me,*" is often left out. As we shall see later, this is clearly very important.

The questions remain, "*Am I responsible for everything that happens to me?*" "*Am I responsible for what I do to myself and to others, based upon what has happened to me?*" I propose that the answer to the first question is a resounding no. We do not always have control over our circumstances, especially as young children or vulnerable adults. Clearly we are not at fault and have not sinned when something beyond our control "happens" to us.

That being said, we must make sure we are faithful in helping adult victims, who have no mental incapacity or other disability, to understand that they are indeed responsible for everything they do, say, and think (as in their responses/reactions to abuse). There are cases where some would say, "*I didn't have a choice.*" But that is not true. You may feel like you did not have a choice, couldn't see or understand your options, or felt you couldn't make a decision, but there is always a choice to be made, and you are the one making it. Therefore, you are responsible. If that choice turns out to be sinful, you are responsible for that sin and the confession and repentance of it. Take, for example, the woman who chooses to seek revenge on her abuser. That is a sinful choice. Or what about the woman who was molested as a child and then chooses to perpetrate the same crimes upon her own children? Would that be sinful and inexcusable? I believe so.

Allow me to provide an illustration that may bring this fact to light. There's a woman who was a victim of childhood physical, verbal, and sexual abuse. Her life and walk with God had not been what it should, or what she desired. She was not raised in a Christian home and did not become a Christian until she became an adult. She didn't feel she was a "bad" person, but she knew she wasn't living up to the high standards God set for His children.

After she married she developed health problems, and after visiting many physicians in her attempt to find answers, she finally found one she thought could help her. Due to the complexity of her medical conditions, she had to have many examinations and, over the course of time, she and the doctor got to know each other fairly well. Then he began behaving in inappropriate ways—saying things to her that didn't sound quite right, making comments on her appearance, taking longer than usual to examine her, and things like that. She thought to herself, "*He's the doctor; he wouldn't do anything to hurt me,*" yet she was still uncomfortable with his change of behavior. Unfortunately, it didn't take long before he became sexually aggressive toward her and one day forced himself on her in his office. Thus began what she thought was an "affair," because she didn't know at the time what professional exploitation through sexual abuse was. The doctor held a fiduciary trust—and he breached it. He had sworn to provide the best care possible to all his patients. He was responsible for helping them heal. He was not supposed to hurt them.

Without going into all the details, suffice it to say God worked to bring her into a position where she could learn the truth about what was happening. He gave her the power to put an end to the ongoing "relationship" and restored her love for, and relationship with, her husband.

Was she completely innocent in this because it was abuse and the one with the power (in this case, the doctor) had the responsibility to protect and do no harm? Some would say yes. She, however, couldn't reconcile that statement with Scripture. How could her husband ever learn to trust her again if at any point in time some person in a role of authority could abuse her? How could she trust herself if she was so vulnerable? Something had to change within her—healing and forgiveness had to take place—for trust to be restored.

While she was very thankful the Lord showed her the truth about what had happened, she didn't have any peace with the thought that she was completely guiltless. The Holy Spirit nagged her until she searched deeper and found truth. The text from 1 Corinthians 10:13 proved to her that help (divine help) was available all along, if she had only clung to that hope and made wise choices based on God's promises rather than giving in and giving up. She had tried to handle the situation on her own. She didn't rely on God's power to help her, and she failed.

She had to admit that while it was *not* an "affair," and the doctor *was* responsible, there was a part for which she was accountable (to God) as well. It was painful for her to admit she had sinned so greatly against God and her husband. It was an adulterous relationship (defined as sex outside of marriage), but it wasn't an affair (defined as a sexual relationship between co-equals). Yes, there *is* a difference. She knew she was guilty of breaking the seventh commandment (Exodus 20:14) and was guilty of lying and deceit—after all, she had to make excuses for meeting with the doctor so frequently and for such long periods of time. Once she realized this, she confessed and sought forgiveness from the Lord and from her husband. Then she said, "*peace like a river, attended my way*" ("It Is Well With My Soul," Horatio G. Spafford, 1873).[7]

So you see, admitting you have sinned and made a mistake, even in the context of an abusive situation as described above, doesn't negate the abuser's responsibility or accountability. Confessing your sins to God frees you to be blessed by Him and to live a more abundant life (John 10:10). Refusing to confess sin—or even refusing to acknowledge any wrongdoing—hinders God from being able to work in your life as He would like.

I believe this applies to all victims—no matter what kind of abuse they may have suffered—if they have resorted to lies, deceit, or anything else God forbids. (I should note here that children and mentally incapacitated adults are *not* usually responsible for sin during any form of abuse.) There can be no forgiveness of sins until we confess and seek forgiveness for our sins.

Most victims are not willing to acknowledge any wrongdoing on their part (if there was any). They want to continue to "play the victim" and gain sympathy (Luke 13:3). What hope, what healing, can exist in remaining a victim? It's better to seek the Lord and allow Him to be the center of our lives. I truly doubt anyone will ever be lost due to seeking forgiveness—even for things in which no forgiveness is necessary. However, some will be lost because they deliberately *failed* to seek forgiveness. If you're in doubt as to whether you had any responsibility or not, pray and ask the Holy Spirit to convict you.

As counselors, we must lovingly and gently help victims to see what their responsibility was in each case, if they had a responsibility, and where they sinned and need to ask for forgiveness. The Lord is gracious and merciful and has promised to pardon our sins. We must claim that promise and hold fast to it (1 John 1:9).

Now let's return to the topic of generational sins. It is important for counselees to be able to understand that while they may have learned certain behaviors from their parents while growing up, they may have had poor examples, they may have been abused in any number of ways, and they may even have inherited (biologically) some less-than-desirable traits or tendencies, they are ultimately responsible for what they choose to do in or with their lives. If they are Christian, then they must understand the verse in Exodus 20:5–6 does not apply to them. They are not "*one who hates the Lord.*" They are re-born as a child of God and, therefore, are no longer under that curse (Exodus 20:6). What a distinction! Yet it is so often overlooked.

Was your father an alcoholic? Were you molested? It doesn't matter what happened to you, God is able to recreate you into His image. Have you been promiscuous? Have you been a liar or adulterer? Have you been a thief or a murderer? Confess your sins to the Lord and trust in His mercy and forgiveness. He is able to restore you into His image and strengthen you to do better—to do His will and not your own. May God help each of us to recognize our sinful natures, regardless of our circumstances, and repent and seek the Lord (2 Corinthians 7:10).

Chapter Nine • Bible Study

Understanding the Victim

Now it's time for some tough questions. Ask yourself the following questions and then answer as honestly as possible. Write down what your plan will be to align your life with the Word of God.

- Am I holding on to the "victim" status to avoid facing some unpleasant change?

____

____

____

____

- Am I avoiding accepting responsibility for my own actions?

____

____

____

____

- Am I allowing God to work within me to perfect my character?

____

____

____

____

- Am I willing to surrender *all* to God and allow Him to be the Lord of my life?

____

____

____

____

Conclusion

Reaching the Hurting—A Biblical Guide for Helping Abuse Victims

It is important for victims to assess their current understanding of salvation through faith (2 Timothy 3:15) and the utmost importance of the atonement of Christ. Jesus is our complete sacrifice (1 Peter 3:18). If we have sinned, then we must seek His forgiveness. We must allow the Holy Spirit to work in our lives to change us into the image of Christ, that we may be partakers of eternal life (Leviticus 19:2; 2 Corinthians 3:18).

Victims must also come to understand the process of sanctification that, as mentioned previously, is the work of a lifetime. An illustration used by Francis Schaeffer in the book *Leaving Yesterday Behind*[8], by Dr. William Hines, is this:

When we look at an iceberg, what we see above water is actually about a tenth of the whole iceberg. That means we don't see 90 percent of what is actually there. This illustration applies to the sin in each of our lives. God knows that we could not bear to see ourselves as we truly are—wretched, miserable, poor, blind, and naked (Revelation 3:17). Therefore, He only reveals to us a little at a time, just what we are able to bear and work on through His grace and power. The sin we see in our lives is only a small percentage of what is actually there. What if we shaved off half of the 10 percent of the iceberg showing above the water? What percentage of the remaining iceberg would we be able to see? The answer is still 10 percent, because as we shave off the top, more of the iceberg floats to the surface; there is always 10 percent showing above the water. So it is with sin. As we work to overcome one thing, God will show us another. We are responsible to deal with sin as it appears in our lives. And there is always sin in our lives. If it appears that there is nothing to change in your life, then you must prayerfully read Psalm 139:23–24, "*Search me, O God, and know my heart: try me, and know my thoughts: And see if there be any wicked way in me, and lead me in the way everlasting.*" God will show you what you need to work on, and He'll give you the strength and power to overcome.

It is not a weakness but a sign of emotional and spiritual maturity to be able to accept responsibility for your own behavior. As counselors, we must show compassion to victims and teach them to look to God for their strength and healing and to take responsibility for their own actions, thoughts, words, and feelings. Blame shifting is never productive. You may have been victimized, but through God's grace you do not need to remain a victim.

Parting Thoughts

- Are you willing to show others biblical truth to facilitate true healing?

____

____

____

____

- Are you willing to trust God to change your heart and life?

____

____

____

____

My prayer is that you will be touched by the Holy Spirit and brought into a deeper, more fulfilling relationship with our Lord and Savior, Jesus Christ.

Endnotes:

1. Dr. William Hines, from course entitled *Counseling the Victim*, November 2003.
2. Dr. Tana Dineen, *Manufacturing Victims: What the Psychology Industry is Doing to People*, Second Edition, 1998.
3. Dr. Tana Dineen, *Manufacturing Victims: What the Psychology Industry is Doing to People*, Second Edition, 1998.
4. Ellen G. White, *Christ's Object Lessons*, 1900.
5. Edith Schaeffer, *Affliction*, August 1993.
6. John J. Murray, *Behind a Frowning Providence*, June 1998.
7. Horatio G. Spafford, "It Is Well With My Soul," 1873.
8. Dr. William Hines, *Leaving Yesterday Behind, A Victim No More*, February 2003.

Notes